Extra Love

DEDICATED TO EVERY FAMILY
WITH A LOVED ONE IN PRISON.

YOU ARE NOT FORGOTTEN.

Hi, my name is Jonathon, and I have a story to tell you, about some really cool things that I learned to do.

2

THIS IS MY LITTLE SISTER, MY DAD AND MY MOTHER.
I LOVE THEM A LOT AND TRY TO BE A GOOD BIG BROTHER.

SOMETIMES WE HAD FUN TOGETHER AND DID COOL STUFF,
BUT BAD STUFF ALSO HAPPENED AND LIFE GOT TOUGH.

THERE WERE TIMES WHEN MY DAD WAS NOT AROUND
AND I THINK MAYBE HE WAS AFRAID
THAT HE COULD NOT GIVE US
WHAT WE NEEDED AND DEAL WITH ALL THE BILLS
THAT HAD TO BE PAID.

BUT I STILL UNDERSTOOD AND IT'S OKAY,
BECAUSE I LOVE HIM VERY MUCH IN EVERY WAY.

WELL, ONE SAD MORNING THE COPS PULLED UP IN FRONT OF OUR YARD. THEY CAME TO THE DOOR AND KNOCKED REALLY HARD.

6

My mom cried, my sister cried and I cried too.
None of us really knew what to do.

I started to miss my dad right away, and was sad he was going to miss my birthday.

SOMETIMES KIDS WERE MEAN AND WOULD POINT AT ME AT SCHOOL. THEY SAID BECAUSE MY DAD WAS IN PRISON, I WAS NOT VERY COOL.

WHEN WE WENT TO VISIT MY DAD THE PRISON WAS FAR AWAY. WE HAD TO GET UP EARLY AND IT TOOK ALL DAY.

So one day, I went by myself to my special spot.
I had to clear my mind and think about a lot.

I knew I couldn't change our situation or make my daddy free,
but maybe things would get better if I could change me.

I LOOKED AT THE BEAUTY OF THE
SUN IN THE SKY,
AND WATCHED THE WAY THE
WILD GEESE FLEW BY.

I THOUGHT, "IF THESE THINGS ARE SO
GOOD THAN GOD MUST BE GOOD TOO,
AND I ASKED HIM TO SHOW ME
WHAT I COULD DO."

17

I REMEMBERED ONE TIME WHEN MY MOM TOLD ME NOT TO PLAY FOOTBALL INSIDE, BUT I DID NOT LISTEN AND WHEN I BROKE HER SPECIAL VASE, SHE CRIED.

I SHOULDN'T HAVE DONE IT AND FELT REALLY BAD, AND I GOT PUNISHED TOO JUST LIKE MY DAD.

I TOOK OUT THE BIBLE THAT GRANDMA GAVE ME AND THERE I READ, ABOUT LOTS OF BEAUTIFUL THINGS THAT GOD SAID.

THAT HE IS OUR FATHER AND WILL BE WITH US EACH DAY,
AND PROMISES TO HEAR US WHENEVER WE PRAY.

20

THAT EVEN THOUGH BAD STUFF HAPPENS AND SOMETIMES WE FEEL REALLY ROTTEN, GOD IS NEAR TO US AND WE ARE NOT FORGOTTEN!

GOD GAVE US EXTRA LOVE WHEN HE GAVE US JESUS, HIS SON
AND IF WE ASK HIM, HE WILL FORGIVE US FOR THE BAD STUFF WE HAVE DONE.

JESUS DiED ON A CROSS FOR YOU AND ME,
BUT THEN HE ROSE AGAiN AND iS ALIVE TODAY, YOU SEE!

SO I THOUGHT, "iF GOD CAN GiVE US SO MUCH,
EVEN THOUGH WE ARE BAD,
THEN I CAN CERTAINLY FORGIVE AND GIVE
EXTRA LOVE TO MY DAD!"

SO I TALKED TO JESUS AND THE FATHER UP ABOVE,
AND ASKED HiM TO GiVE ME HiS SPECiAL LOVE.

23

I REALIZED THAT MY DADDY WAS SAD AND HURTING INSIDE, BUT I COULD HELP HIM BY PUTTING GOOD THOUGHTS IN HIS MIND.

SO I WENT BACK TO MY SPECIAL SPOT AND SAT ON THE GROUND. I TOOK A NOTEBOOK AND WROTE SOME IDEAS DOWN.

ABOUT WAYS I COULD HELP MY FAMILY AND THINGS I COULD DO, TO BRING US TOGETHER AND BE THE GLUE!

Extra Love For Dad :

1.) Tell him I forgive him and love him.

2.) Work on a story together.

3.) Make him laugh.

4.) Play the game I made up with him.

5.) Start a special club with him.

6.) Have a talent show together.

7.) Tell him the bible verse I memorized to encourage him.

Extra Love for Mom:

1.) Give her lots of hugs.

2.) Wash the dishes and clean the house.

3.) Buy her flowers for no reason.

4.) Tell her she is special and I love her.

Extra Love for My Sister:

1.) Play with her whatever she wants.

2.) Tell a story in the bible to her.

3.) Buy her a little present.

NOW, I WAS LOOKING FORWARD TO VISITING MY DAD FOR THE VERY FIRST TIME,
BECAUSE I WAS BRINGING HIM SOMETHING SPECIAL LIKE A SONG AND A RHYME.

THE PRISON WASN'T SO SCARY NOW BECAUSE I HAD GOD'S LOVE TO GIVE,
AND WHEN YOU LOVE SOMEONE ELSE, LIFE IS MUCH BETTER TO LIVE.

WE PRETENDED THAT THE PRISON WAS INSTEAD A CASTLE, AND I DIDN'T MIND WAITING OR ANY OF THE HASSLE.

IT DIDN'T BOTHER ME WHAT ANYONE ELSE SAID OR THOUGHT, BECAUSE TO ALWAYS FORGIVE IS WHAT JESUS TAUGHT.

27

NO MATTER WHAT, WE CAN CHOOSE OUR ATTITUDE AND HAVE A BIG HEART, AND BRING OUR FAMILY TOGETHER EVEN IF WE ARE APART.

YOU CAN MAKE A LIST HERE OF SPECIAL IDEAS TO DO, WITH YOUR PARENT IN PRISON JUST FROM YOU!

REMEMBER TO ALWAYS TALK TO OUR FATHER ABOVE, AND ASK JESUS TO GIVE YOU HIS EXTRA LOVE!

Ideas I can do to give Extra Love to my parent in prison:

1.)

2.)

3.)

4.)

5.)

6.)

7.)

8.)

Made in United States
Troutdale, OR
03/19/2025